Tamicka,
I pray that you are
blessed by reading this
as much as I was in writing it!
Multiplied blessing to you!

Denita
July 2015

HAPPY BIRTHDAY
GOD BLESS
YOU
Raquel
7-30-15

Managing Up: Doing It God's Way

Becoming a Spirit-Led Assistant

Venita L. Blakely

WESTBOW®
PRESS
A DIVISION OF THOMAS NELSON
& ZONDERVAN

Scripture quotations are taken from the King James Version (KJV) and the Amplified Version (Amp) are taken from the *King James Version/Amplified Bible Parallel Edition*, published by Zondervan, Grand Rapids Michigan 49530, USA.

Amplified Bible copyright 1954, 1958, 1962, 1964, 1965, 1987 by The Lockman Foundation

Scripture quotations denoted the Message Version are taken from *The Message Bible*. Copyright 1993, 1994, 1995, 1996, 2000, 2001, 2002. Used by permission of NavPress Publishing Group. Colorado Springs Colorado 80920, USA.

WestBow Press books may be ordered through booksellers or by contacting:

WestBow Press
A Division of Thomas Nelson & Zondervan
1663 Liberty Drive
Bloomington, IN 47403
www.westbowpress.com
1 (866) 928-1240

ISBN: 978-1-4908-7451-7 (sc)
ISBN: 978-1-4908-7452-4 (e)

Library of Congress Control Number: 2015904872

Print information available on the last page.

WestBow Press rev. date: 4/30/2015

Contents

Acknowledgements

I want to thank my Pastors Creflo and Taffi Dollar for being my spiritual parents. Since they took the charge to become "students of Grace," I accepted the charge to be a "carrier of Grace." Their teachings on Grace has allowed me to begin living my life understanding how God empowers me to prosper and that it is His undeserved, unmerited favor brought about by His love for me that allows me to realize the unlimited possibilities I am now experiencing!

I thank my boss, Minister Ken Terry for providing me the opportunity to serve him as I serve Christ. It has been his faith in me that created opportunities for growth and development in ways that I never thought I would experience. This book is borne out of my working relationship with him.

As I sought ways to improve myself and performance, I learned about this concept while speaking with Minister Vic Bolton. Thank you for introducing me to "Managing Up". God used you to take me to the next level.

As always, my children are never to be left out, Nicole, Nathan and Lauren: you inspire me to always do better than before.

And I cannot ever leave out my Lord and Savior, Jesus Christ. It is because of him and his finished work that I get to experience a life that only exists in Him. It's called Kingdom living!

Foreword

"Managing Up: Doing It God's Way" is a book that is long overdue to those who operate in the gift of Administration. Venita Blakely has served as my Executive Assistant for years now and I've seen firsthand her sensitivity to the Holy Spirit's leading as she carries out her tasks. No, I'm not saying that she breaks out into tongues in the middle of a meeting or states "Thus saith the Lord" before giving me an answer to a question. I'm expressing how she operates in wisdom, knowledge, integrity, honor, respect and hard work. These are Spirit-led traits. Venita is a "problem solver" and, in my world where I'm faced with challenges and problems every day, she's invaluable. She makes me look good.

For the Supervisor, Manager or Director who's seeking a Spirit-led Assistant, this book will help you to know what to look for in an Assistant. For the Assistant who's looking to become a Spirit-led Assistant, this book will show you how to do just that. I believe that this book is paving a new avenue in the area of Christian Administration and is the first of many that will help further the Kingdom of God.

You will be blessed by reading *"Managing Up: Doing It God's Way"*. If you're currently an Assistant, take these principles that Venita has shared in this book and allow the Holy Spirit to make them yours. As for me, Venita is my Spirit-led Assistant. Enjoy!

Minister Ken Terry
Director, Ministry Affairs & Outreach
World Changers Church International

Introduction

"Managing Up" the definition:

1. To build a successful working relationship with a superior, manager, or employer (Dictionary.com) 2. Positioning others in a positive light. It is a form of communication that aligns your skills with that of your boss 3. Doing your job in a way that makes your boss' job easier.

"Managing Up" is a term commonly used in Corporate America to describe the working relationship between a manager and an assistant. It has gained popularity in recent years. The primary basis of "managing up" is one's attitude in the working relationship with one's boss and how that attitude determines the performance while working with and for that boss. Some highlights of "Managing Up" are:

1. Paying attention to your boss' needs
2. It's proactive and will seek out ways to improve the workplace and processes
3. You become a team player – doing whatever it takes to get the job done

4. Your needs are met by meeting your boss' needs
5. Managing Up is a way to make you stand out in the workplace

The bottom line is that you are doing whatever is necessary to make your boss look good. You make him look good by making his job easier to perform. If he is successful, then you are successful.

I learned about "Managing Up" after working in a position as an Executive Assistant. After a year on the job, I began to evaluate my performance and although I knew I was doing a good job, I was looking for ways to improve my skills and set new goals for the job. I began researching and asking around and happened to talk with one of the ministers at the church I work at. He works in public relations and asked if I'd ever heard the term before. That was all I needed. As that call ended, I went online and looked it up and ended up buying books, and one in particular, "Managing Up" by Rosanne Badowski, really made an impact on me. As I began to incorporate some of the principles she wrote about, into my work performance, Holy Spirit spoke to me and shared that I had been "managing up" all along during my work life. He told me that Badowski's book just brought it to the forefront. When I asked Him how the book influenced me at that level, He reminded me of the scripture I have been using for years and is still the foundation for my work ethic. It is Colossians 3:20-24, specifically, verse 23. It says:

"And whatsoever ye do, do it heartily, as to the Lord, and not unto men..." (KJV)

The Amplified version of the full passage is stated below:

"Servants, obey in everything those who are your earthly masters, not when their eyes are on you as pleasers of men, but in simplicity of purpose [with all your heart] because of your reverence for the Lord and as a sincere expression of your devotion to Him. Whatever may be your task, work at it heartily (from the soul), as [something done] for the Lord and not for men, knowing [with all certainty] that it is from the Lord [and not from men] that you will receive the inheritance which is your [real] reward. [The One Whom] you are actually serving [is] the Lord Christ (the Messiah)."

I first read this scripture in the 80's and when I did, my work ethic changed significantly. My entire perspective concerning the job I was working on, changed completely. My only concern was to please God because I was performing that job as unto Him. I decided I was going to do my job as I was led by the Holy Spirit. Studying this scripture, Holy Spirit began to show me that although I had been applying this to my professional life; the full understanding of what it meant came recently. I came to realize that as I performed my job "heartily" I was working on it until it was completed; I was going above and beyond what was expected of me. I looked up the word, "heartily" in the Greek translation of the Strong's Concordance, and it means, "exceedingly, to completion", and "spirit, breath." Just as Jesus said in Matthew 4:4 that, "Man does not live by bread alone, but by every Word that proceeds out of the mouth of God," my response to this scripture has been that as He gave me instructions or showed me how to do a certain job, I listened and my performance usually exceeded expectations. As a Christian, my relationship with Jesus Christ is enhanced because I have accepted the help and guidance of the Holy Spirit. Jesus said in St. John 16:13 that He would send us a Comforter, one who would not only lead us but guide and teach us. As I would pray and ask for guidance and direction, the Holy Spirit would show me how to do certain things that pertained to my job. That guidance and direction took me beyond what I was accustomed to; usually outside of my comfort zone. To take it further, I was allowing Holy Spirit to SHOW me and TEACH me how to do my job. I was giving God permission to enter into my "work life." "Not by might, nor by power, but by His Spirit" was I going to perform my job(s) moving forward. (See Zechariah 4:6)

Because of my attitude and mindset being as such, God ultimately promoted me to serve a senior director for one of the largest mega churches of our time. I have been humbled with this assignment because as I submitted to the Holy Spirit, the position I'm in currently is one that I know I was not qualified for in terms of skills or education but one of extreme favor from God.... and man. To be his executive assistant has been an awesome experience, never a dull moment; especially when I realized that the departments this man has been entrusted with affects the overall membership of the church in some capacity – that's some 30,000 members!

Over the years and working in this present position, the Holy Spirit has given me insight in performing all of my tasks, regardless how big or small those tasks were. I have learned a few things that I have shared with others and now I believe God wants me to share those things to a broader audience. There is a way to be in a supportive role and give God all the glory in your present position. As a follower, I've become a leader.

CHAPTER 1

Capture the Vision

Habakkuk 2:2 says, "....write the vision, and engrave it so plainly upon tablets that everyone that passes may be able to read it quickly and easily as he hastens by." (Amplified version)

We all know that working in any organization, knowing the vision and/or mission is very important as it helps us know what we are working towards. The senior leadership is responsible for ensuring the execution of the vision through the departments they have oversight of. This can be somewhat challenging when your senior director has several departments to oversee. Although there are managers running the departments, the senior director has to ensure his managers are operating with the vision in mind.

As the assistant, your role may consist of ensuring that the vision is being fulfilled by following up on assignments given to the managers. Following up on assignments – checking on the status, understanding of expectations, answering questions – availing oneself to help out in any way possible. Part of your responsibilities may be to ensure that timelines are met and assignments turned in on time. Additional responsibilities may consist of working on projects with other departments; calling upon the other executive assistants or secretaries to help get resolution to any hindrances to a given assignment – calling them to find out the status of an item, give them any background information to help them identify it and bring it to their administrator's attention in order to get the item resolved and keep the process moving.

"As a man thinks in his heart, so is he" (Proverbs 23:7) and " ...out of the abundance of the heart, man speaks." (Matthew 12:34) In order to help your director fulfill the vision, you have to not only know the vision, but also get full of it. Your attitude, behavior, conversation, is to be such that others will know that you are focused, "working on a mission". Look at your areas and seek God as to how you are to fulfill your part of the vision. As you understand how your boss' departments interact and overlap with each other, you become mindful and more strategic in how you perform your tasks and how you relate with any customers, clients, and guests – internally and externally.

My boss' departments all encompass the direct contact of people (our members, primarily) in one form or another. Knowing this, I realized that we had to be mindful of how we treat each member who called, wrote, or came to the ministry to have a specific need met. That is only a part of what takes place in our office; he also travels extensively with the CEO and they have a very close relationship. When I realized what I had signed up for, my prayer became, "Lord, how do You want me to do this job? How do You want me to not only be effective but be a blessing to him and the organization?"

I learned to listen and what to follow up on. When certain statements were made, I learned that those statements would eventually become an assignment and took note of it. The same happened with my boss. In meetings, as I took notes, I would highlight the ones to follow up. Those notes eventually became compartmentalized: sharing current info/status updates; potential action items, and definite action items.

That's when I realized that I was not only called to be a part of this organization; I was on "assignment." Not only am I on assignment, there are several things that the Holy Spirit has given me an awareness to that as I perform my tasks, I make sure I meet those areas or objectives daily. I realized that I'm in this current position "on purpose" and that it is not a coincidence that I was selected for this position. There is a much bigger picture than the office I work out of. The directive is more than I ever imagined. Since I've been in this position, I've had to fine tune some "skills" that I will discuss in some detail in the following chapters.

CHAPTER 2

Pray for Those Over You....Literally

Realizing I was on assignment, my personal prayer life changed. My prayers became more fervent and more strategic. The time of praying in generalities was over. I began to pray for my boss. The Bible says to "pray for those who have rule over you, and for those who watch over your souls. (Hebrews 13:17). I realize the scripture speaks to authority figures (Pastors) but the same principle applies here. They are responsible for your well-being and are held accountable for you. Early in my tenure, I mentioned to my boss that I realized that outside of the CEO's position, he had the greatest level of responsibility because he was entrusted with over 30,000 "souls." Every department he oversees touches the lives of the members in some form or fashion. My boss' response, although humbling, was every part of the organization was "interdependent" of each other and went on to explain. Although I understood what he said, I knew better.

My view changed regarding how I did my job. I sought ways to not only improve my performance, the structure of the office, but most of all, streamline the processes so that he could fulfill his assignment in assisting the CEO in fulfilling his assignment. When you realize that your boss has an assignment, you approach your job differently. I realized that he and I were a team and I had a significant effect on his success, or failure, in fulfilling his assignment.

With that in mind, each piece of paper that came into the office did not always land on his desk. Every concern or problem did not enter his office. I began to pay attention to every detail, taking the time to go over each issue. Every manager did not have the level of access they were accustomed to before I came because I knew he was on assignment. When we talked, I began listening with my inner ear, picking up his way of thinking, asking questions when needed for clarity and understanding. I literally became the gatekeeper and his Intercessor while on the job.

As I continued to pray and intercede for my boss, there were times of extended prayer, times when I spent prolonged periods praying for him. I hope you, as the reader, will understand the next comment I'm going to make; I will preface the statement by saying that I realized that in doing this job, it was not going to be an easy task and truthfully, the assignment was, and still is, much bigger, than myself. When I pray for him I always pray in tongues: the Holy Spirit knows what to pray for and prays the perfect will of God. Not only is that true, it also builds us up in our most holy faith. (Romans 8:26, Jude 20) Praying in tongues positions you to see and hear things differently; it is as if you are functioning at another level and you are. You're functioning from the "inside out." Not allowing the outward circumstances or situations to influence you but you operate from what is known as your spirit (God-created self). You know it better as your intuition or conscience.

In spending time praying in tongues, the Holy Spirit sometimes gave me the words to speak in my understanding and I would speak and pray those words. Most of the time was spent praying in tongues until I received a level of peace in my spirit. This continues today. (I don't think he realizes this is what I do). :-)

Every time I've spent praying in tongues for my boss, it has netted immediate results. Usually later in the day when he and I have opportunity to meet, he'll go over his notes from his senior level meetings and then informs me of whatever new assignment he's been given and the details of that assignment. Of course this means the assignment is mine to research and becomes a new project. One time he came out of a meeting and as he walked into his office he told me, "Well, Venita, I need to find out how to harvest and store grain." I looked up from my computer and said, "Joseph?" "Yes" was his reply. I started laughing because I knew nothing about farming! I am a city girl - born and raised. The only time I was remotely close to a farm was when my sisters and I would spend time in Arkansas visiting my grandparents and their neighbors owned a pig farm!

While he went into his office, I sat at my desk and looked up, thinking "My God, are we getting ready to own a farm?" I remembered the story of Joseph in the Bible (Genesis chapters 39-45) and immediately prayed, "Lord, I need your help; I have no clue as to how to begin this process. Please show me where to start." As I sat at my computer, Google™ sat waiting for me to enter SOMEthing.... Long story short, I made phone calls, spent hours searching online, was willing to visit farmers who were nearby in order to help fulfill his assignment. All this happened in less than two weeks' time. By the time he made his presentation in his meeting with the senior team, I was pretty well versed in farm machinery, testing the soil, the process of storing grain, what type of storage is available and the minimum amount of grain you could store. The startup costs alone? Let's just say, farming ain't cheap!

The information was presented to the senior leadership shortly thereafter. The last thing I knew, some acreage was set aside to begin farming on behalf of the ministry. This helps to fulfill the part of the vision that states, ".....making a mark (in the lives of people) that cannot be erased."

When you pray for your boss, the results are immediate. It positions you to be a greater asset to him because you're seeing and hearing differently than the average assistant. Your senses are heightened, looking for any and every opportunity to maximize, execute, enforce, streamline, and implement whatever is necessary to make him look good.

When you pray in the Holy Spirit, the Bible say that He prays the perfect prayer. There will be times and situations where you will have no idea how to complete an assignment, especially when you're working in a forward or progressive organization. Praying in tongues positions you to hear and receive differently than you may be accustomed to. It provides an opportunity for you to stop relying on yourself and your efforts, and rely on His Spirit to lead you. When you do this, an idea, solution, way to do something, additional instructions, the next step in a process, will suddenly reveal itself and you realize that that additional insight has made it easier to do the particular task for that time. God wants us to rely on Him in doing our jobs and when we do, it becomes easier; we actually begin to enjoy doing what we do.

When do you know you need to pray?

1. When you're trying to learn your boss' ways and how he makes decisions
2. When you're given an assignment and you have no clue how to start it
3. When you need the right words to say
4. When it becomes "intense" in the office
5. To keep the right attitude
6. All the time! Be instant in season and out of season and Men ought to always pray!

There may be some of you reading this and wondering how do I pray in tongues? You may have some philosophical differences where praying in tongues is concerned but I want to provide some understanding about tongues. Praying in tongues is a gift from God and He gives it freely to those who ask Him for it. The only condition is that you have to be born-again. That's right, you have to accept Jesus into your heart and you do that by believing what He did on the cross was for your benefit. Jesus came to take all of our bad, so that we could have all of his good. Every good and perfect gift comes from the Father above and everything Jesus has for us is good. We were created in His image and after His likeness. This means that we are first of all, a spirit. We have a soul, and we live in a body. Our spirit is what God created as a place that He alone is to live, reside. It is that place in us where we previously looked to anything and everyone else to fill that place but only God can live there and bring us the life that He originally created for us. There is a life that we are to live and it is totally opposite of what we live with on a daily basis. Where there is envy, strife, competition, God has love, acceptance, wholeness and peace. Each one of us has been created uniquely different and each aspect of us is to reflect who God is while we are on this earth.

To accept this gift of Jesus is to receive salvation. Salvation in this aspect means, wholeness, healing, health, prosperity, deliverance. It's more inwardly that eventually shows up outwardly. To accept this gift, please say these words aloud:

"Father God, thank you for Jesus. Thank you that He came to take away all of my bad so that I could have all of His good. He died for me so that I can live. I accept what Jesus did for me and ask Him to come into my heart and save me. I believe Him and thank Him for salvation. Thank you Jesus! Amen."

Now to receive the gift of tongues:

"Father God, before Jesus died, He said that He would not leave us without comfort and that He would send the Holy Ghost who would not only comfort us but teach us, lead us, and guide us. To receive the gift of the Holy Ghost, I acknowledge that I have accepted and received Jesus as my Lord and Savior. I want this gift of the Holy Ghost and the physical evidence of receiving this gift is by speaking in tongues. Baptize me, in Jesus' name. I receive the baptism by faith in Jesus' name; I believe I receive and the first syllable that comes to my mind, I speak it and keep saying it. Praise the Lord, thank you Jesus for this wonderful gift!"

In receiving the baptism of the Holy Ghost, you may feel a warming sensation come over you and whatever syllable that comes to mind, say it no matter how inconsequential you think it may be. Do not be afraid, just believe and trust. The lovely thing about it all is that you can start and stop the syllables whenever you want. There's nothing spooky about receiving the gift. The lovely thing about God is that He's given us free will, meaning He's given us the freedom of choice. We can choose to accept Him and what he's made available to us, or we can choose NOT to receive....it's up to us. Personally, it's been the best decision I've ever made; my life has not been the same and I'm glad about it!

CHAPTER 3

How to be a Blessing, Not a Curse

As a woman, I am by nature a nurturer. I am also a helpmeet suitable. Although these statements have usually applied to marriage and family, I have found these characteristics very helpful in my present position. As a nurturer, I protect my boss, in one of two ways. I protect the atmosphere in the office by ensuring that it is conducive to not only productivity, but also creativity. The office is positioned to accomplish whatever project, task, assignment or aspect in doing whatever is necessary to bring about the desired results. I protect him by screening whoever is trying to get close or access to him through the numerous requests made to see him on a daily basis. Everyone does not have the same level of access to him as others may have. A definition of helpmeet that I really like and I believe is fitting in this setting: "companion, helper, anything that aids or assists; helper who is right for him/her.

An example: I remember at the end of my interview, I asked the Holy Spirit if there was anything else I needed to share in order to get this job. He reminded me of how I've always added my strength to whomever I was working with and wanted me to share that tidbit of information. I asked my director if I could share one last thing and he gave me permission to speak. As I relayed this information, I had to control the intonations in my voice and I became teary-eyed. I felt the power of God come over me, evidenced by my voice cracking and when my director stopped working. He was writing and as I began to share, he stopped writing and lowered his head as if to say, "Finally! Someone who's able to help me complete my assignment!" Because I was able to "see" the magnitude of his responsibilities, I also saw that he didn't have an adequate support system at that time, the Holy Spirit allowed me to share a key piece of information that would be of great benefit to him. I didn't realize it at the time but I was already exhibiting a key trait in "managing up"...

I begin each day positioning myself to be a blessing. I spend time in prayer, worship, and the Word of God. I go into work with an attitude that says, "I can do all things through Christ, who gives me the strength." (Philippians 4:19). I go into work determined to receive any instructions I need to complete my tasks, from the Holy Spirit. There has not been a time (that I can remember) when I did not solicit the Holy Spirit's help in performing my job. I cannot complete this assignment without the help of the Holy Spirit. In doing this, I am able to go to work with the joy of The Lord in my heart and I go to work expecting nothing but good to take place. One of the things I pray regularly is that God would "season my speech with salt and grace so I will have an answer to give every man." (Colossians 4:6). That means that my conversation is pleasant and my response will be such that I build up the person or team I am speaking with. My conversation with others will not be offensive or have an attitude attached to it. I am swift to hear and slow to speak; I listen more than I talk. I listen, making sure I understand the person talking and when I'm not certain, I ask questions until I understand. At the same time, when I talk with the team, I share with them my reasons for the inquiries. Any questions they have, I should have an answer. This helps them gain further clarity in their assignments. Being in the position I'm in, I realize the weight of the responsibility and authority I carry. I don't take it lightly, either.

Side note: Being in this position, I have to watch my mouth; watch what I say. There is so much information that flows in and out of this office and a significant portion is confidential. Not only do I maintain strict confidentiality when I speak with other staff, I use wisdom and discretion in speaking with them. I don't share everything with everybody. I stated earlier that every piece of paper or communication did not go across my director's desk. I use discretion when it comes to sharing information with him. Because he oversees eight (8) departments, every challenge that comes up does not get his attention; he has managers in place to address those challenges. Our office is made aware of every situation via email (and sometimes a phone call if it is serious) and I will usually follow that conversation and will ask questions if necessary. What ends up happening is that when he and I finally sit down to discuss any action items or daily activities, the situation/challenge will come up and then I will basically give him the highlights of what caused the challenge and any resolution. There are times when I'll brief him as a "just so you know" so that he'll be aware and have some familiarity about the situation, especially if it has been occurring for some time.

Communication is very important in working with and for my senior director....and to his managers. Because so much information flows in and out of our office, we do not always have the opportunity to meet regularly. A lot of our communication takes place just before he goes to his meeting with the senior team and at the end of the day. I am thankful for technology though, especially text messaging. Outside of the phone, I have "involuntarily" recruited my director into the world of text messaging. Whenever an item of importance comes up - unscheduled meeting, situation that needs to be addressed immediately, whatever - I usually inform him via text message. Mind you, this takes place when he's out of the office. The text message is usually my first "step" in reaching out to him. To give you an idea of how I communicate when a situation comes up, I: 1. Send a text message to alert him of the situation 2. Forward/ email him the overview of the situation so he has a frame of reference. 3. Wait for his response. When he responds to my text message, I know he is reviewing everything in the email and has probably called the manager involved to find out more details. Someone may be saying, "Why didn't you call at the onset of the situation?" This process has worked primarily because he is usually travelling and the majority of the time, he is not available to speak by phone. There have been instances where the situation was urgent that I did call initially and left a voice message but I still followed up with a text message to let him know I left him a voice message. I know he'll read the text message before listening to the voice message. Let me also add that I am still communicating with the manager, receiving any updates, offering recommendations or potential solutions. By the time I hear from him, I will provide the latest updates, instructions for resolution if it hasn't been resolved by the time we speak. In communicating with your boss, it is very important to establish a method of communicating that will work for both of you.

I remember my second year on the job and he was on vacation. He and I would communicate a certain time each day unless an emergency came up and after exhausting any and all possibilities, I'd reach out to him. This vacation, he called me to tell me that he'd schedule a conference call and wanted me to facilitate the call. Later that morning, one of our staff persons came over to tell me of a situation that would have an immediate adverse impact on the weekly operations. As I was conveying the information to my boss, he elected to address that situation personally and wanted me to take over the conference call. Again, Holy Spirit, help me! I didn't know anything about the subject matter outside of what I researched for the conference call and here I was, getting ready to facilitate and actually navigate the conference call! The Holy Spirit directed the questions, guided me through unfamiliar territory and the overall outcome of that initial conference call? Through a series of meetings with government officials, a law was successfully implemented where nonprofit organizations cannot be sued for donations received if they were received in good faith. This law was borne out of Ponzi schemes that have been in the news over the last several years. Because the church operates primarily on tithes and offerings from its members, our pastor wanted to ensure that not only our ministry but other nonprofits and churches, would not be affected by receiving monies in good faith. So this was an assignment given to my director and I was tasked with the researching and follow through.

What I learned out of this experience was that although I'd only been in this position for less than two years, my director trusted me enough and was comfortable enough to place me in the position to lead this conference call and be as involved in the process to bring it to fruition. There is a scripture that says, "...the servant refreshes the soul of his master..." (Proverbs 25:13). This means that the master has entrusted his spirit (heart) to his servant. His performance, assignment, outcome has been entrusted to another person – the one walking alongside him in completing God's plan, mission. The master has faith, he believes that the servant has his interests in mind as he goes about his daily activities and because he believes this about his servant, he is confident about the activities his servant is involved in. He knows that those activities his servant is involved in will yield positive results and he (the master) will be pleased and satisfied. To take it further, as a Spirit-led Assistant, as you follow the leading of the Holy Spirit, your boss becomes more effective at doing his job. He is more alert, more capable and comes up with new ideas without any stress because of you. You keep the flow of the office moving and your boss doesn't have to stop and revisit projects or assignments. He has a calm about himself because he knows that his assistant is doing her job.

The best example of this is the story of Joseph in Genesis chapters 35-39. What sticks out about Joseph is that at the outset of this passage, the bible says that "the Lord was with him." In the short time of working with my director, there's been enough evidence or fruit as I like to call it, that he felt comfortable enough and trusted me enough to initiate this process.

With the signing of the bill into law, there is now a precedent established and we are now positioned to approach each state where we have a Satellite church and start the process of reaching out to the lawmakers in those states and get a similar law established there. That is awesome and God has allowed me to be a part of all of this! I am deeply humbled and honored.

CHAPTER 4

The Greatest is Servant: A Lesson in Humility (Highlighting Jesus)

Jesus said in Matthew 23:11 "But he who is greatest among you shall be your servant." Servant in the Greek means pastor, deacon, and attendant. In the passage of scripture, Jesus was talking with the people and referencing the Pharisees of the day. They enjoyed being the center of attention everywhere they went. He tells the people to go ahead and observe whatever the Pharisees say to observe, but don't do what they do. These leaders are empty, self-centered, and only want to be seen and recognized for the positions they're in.

Because "servant" means pastor, deacon, attendant, I'm reminded of what they do. Another name for Pastor is

Shepherd and he is responsible for taking care of the sheep. He makes sure they are fed and watered daily, kept clean and healthy, and finally, protected from any harm or danger. The shepherd directs them and uses the rod that he carries all the time. That same rod is used for different purposes. Deacons serve: they visit the sick and widows and those who may not be able to leave home for extended periods of time. In Acts 6, it speaks about how there were seven (7) men selected to assist in providing relief to the widows.

Taking the definitions above and applying to our position: As an assistant, we serve our bosses. Although we may not be in a "leadership" capacity (and I say this loosely), our focus or primary responsibility is one of providing relief to our bosses. Every task, every assignment, every responsibility we have, is to ensure our boss is able to operate in his role at an optimum level. Although he has the responsibility of several departments and has put the vision or mission or objectives before the team, as the assistant, (and I would like to take some liberty here) we can be considered as "the rod" that is used to help guide and direct the team. Just as that rod the shepherd carries is used to guide and direct the sheep by gently prodding them in a certain direction - towards a higher elevation, whether for food or for protection. The rod can also be used as a weapon to protect the sheep from any (un)foreseen dangers. In like manner, as assistants, we encourage the team by reminding them of the direction we are to move in by the instructions given by our director. By coaching, encouraging them, we help take them to a higher "ground" by taking them to a higher level of productivity in their assignment. This helps provide the "relief" for bosses because they do not have to physically oversee the day-to-day operations of their departments. As their assistants, we're working "behind the scenes" ensuring the managers have what they need to meet their objectives.

As Holy Spirit-led assistants, we have our ears and eyes open, always aware of the activities taking place in and around the departments your boss oversees. As the "rod" to your boss, you may speak with a manager about an employee to bring attention to an issue before it gets any bigger. By speaking with the manager, you help to guide and assist by making sure he is aware of a potential situation before it becomes a situation. You constantly have the bigger picture in mind as you interact with others and more importantly, you "see" how your boss' assignment fits into the overall scope of the organization. As you speak to any of the managers, you may offer suggestions that can help improve performance or become more efficient. You may have noticed or become aware of, an employee, or another assistant, who, in their effort to do well in their position, became overwhelmed by taking on more tasks than they're capable of completing. Although he may think he's a team player, until he completes an assignment successfully, he has the potential of becoming a source of frustration to the rest of the staff. This can result in sub par work, affecting the boss' performance. By staying mindful about your boss' assignment, keep the lines of communication open with the managers and share as necessary in order to help keep the operations flowing smoothly.

Jesus came as a servant. The Message translation of Matthew says, "Do you want to stand out? Then step down. Be a servant. If you puff yourself up, you'll get the wind knocked out of you. But if you're content to be yourself, your life will count for plenty." Jesus understood His role, and followed the instructions of His "boss", Jehovah God. He understood His assignment in the earth. He chose to take on human flesh to save mankind from their sins by ultimately dying on the cross. He chose to give up his heavenly position and come on this planet so that not only could we be in constant fellowship with Him but we are able to sit in heavenly places with him too. Jesus humbled himself and in the end, He was exalted KING of KINGS and LORD of LORDS. There is no greater name in heaven or in earth than the name of Jesus. And it's all because He made a decision to humble himself in order to fulfill the assignment given to him by his Father, God. Because Jesus humbled himself, who are we, that we can't humble ourselves to our bosses in order for the vision to be fulfilled?

Titus 3:1 speaks to subjecting ourselves to the principalities and authorities that exist and be willing, able, and ready to do every good, honorable work. We subject ourselves by submitting or getting under, obedience (by getting under the mission). Whatever task or responsibility given to us, as spirit-led assistants, we're willing, able, and ready to do the task and do it honorably. We bring honor to God by our obedience to our boss. I know this may be a strange concept; people have an issue with the word "obedience" but as a spirit-led assistant, everything you do is done out of your relationship with Christ. Jesus didn't do anything until His Father told him what, how, and when to do it. Jesus didn't think anything about a subject until God TOLD him how to think about the subject! (See St. John5:30). The source of Jesus' humility was his relationship with his Father, God. As we're mindful of our relationship with Christ, we serve alongside our boss with the same attitude and eventually, promotion comes.

CHAPTER 5

Whatsoever You Do, Do it as Unto The Lord!

"So if you're serious about living this new resurrection life with Christ, *act* like it. Pursue the things over which Christ presides. Don't shuffle along, eyes to the ground, absorbed with the things right in front of you. Look up, and be alert to what is going on around Christ – that's where the action is. See things from *his* perspective." (Colossians 3:1, 2 The Message) The Amplified version says to "set your minds and keep them set on what is above (the higher things), not on the things that are on the earth." I've stated earlier that as you allow yourself to be led by the Holy Spirit you give Him permission to teach you, lead you, and guide you. As the process takes place, your thinking changes; you begin to think differently.

This new way of thinking causes you to approach your job differently.

As I looked up the words "set" and "affection" in the Greek, they mean the same thing: *to interest oneself,* and *be of the same understanding.* In order to interest oneself, you have to engage yourself so that changes will take place. Those changes won't come unless you become interested in changing your thoughts as to how you perform your job. In other words, as you "set" yourself, you have the same understanding, same sentiment; follow the same thought, as your boss. You interest yourself or engage yourself. You elevate yourself by your attitude and the way you carry yourself. Your approach to your job is completely different because you are not going through the motions, pushing paper for eight (8) hours a day. You are intentional in every task that you work on. Everything you do is on purpose. You have a reason and an end in mind; you see the purpose and end result in everything you accomplish. You have elevated your thinking, mentality, attitude, and mindset, from a worker bee - just do what I have to because I have to - to one of wanting to do my best at all times - "I am here for a reason, and what I do is making an impact towards fulfilling the vision of this organization." You work with purpose and on purpose. When your thought processes become changed to this level, your entire demeanor changes. The way you carry yourself and interact with others, changes. Your conversation changes, your responses and actions change.

As I think about this, I can remember when I first started working as an Executive Assistant and one of the first things I set out to do was learn how my boss did his job. I wanted to know how he thought, the process he used to reach his decisions for approval, how he managed his departments, everything I could know in order to assist him fully and help him maximize his potential. When I learned what he looked for before approving items, I spoke with his managers and asked them to include certain items when presenting budgets and/or memos for approval. This minimized the time it took to approve the requests because any potential questions were answered before they were asked. He had the information he needed at the onset instead of making a phone call or sending the request back because of insufficient information.

I believe Joseph is the perfect example, outside of Jesus, in depicting true servant hood. No matter what Joseph was assigned to do, he remained faithful to the dream/vision God gave him. (See Genesis 37). In the 39th chapter of Genesis, the story picks up with Joseph serving an officer to Pharaoh and because he was lied upon by the wife of the officer, he was sent to prison. The bible says before that took place "that the Lord was with Joseph and he was a prosperous man." (verse 2). Due to Potiphar's wife lusting after Joseph and his continuous refusal of her advances, at some point, she got angry with him and lied to her husband and was sent to prison. In spite of what seemed to be a "setback" Joseph remained faithful to the dream God gave him. He did not allow the prison to limit what he knew as his ultimate destiny. With the job he had in prison, he performed it in such a way that he was ultimately promoted to be the one responsible for all of the prisoners' wellbeing. I want to interject here how his story applies to "managing up": when he was serving in Potiphar's house, he became the overseer of everything Potiphar owned. He was entrusted with the full operation of Potiphar's house and staff. He performed that job in such a way that Potiphar had NO IDEA what he owned; he gave Joseph FULL RESPONSIBILITY over everything he had with two exceptions: his food and his wife. He was faithful over whatever "assignment" was given to him, he followed the instructions Potiphar gave and fulfilled those instructions to completion. This allowed him to bear fruit no matter where he was. While he was in prison, promotion came. It came because "the Lord was with him" in everything he encountered. What was his promotion, you ask? Joseph ultimately became the second in command to the Pharoah of Egypt! To sum up Joseph's experiences:

- *He knew Potiphar's expectations/vision*
- *He stayed focused* – Joseph went to work every day and concentrated on the duties of the day. He was not distracted by his boss' wife's comments and advances.
- *He knew his limitations, boundaries* – When she grabbed him, he ran out of his coat of many colors and RAN!
- *He was able to give an answer to every man who inquired of him* -- He was able to interpret the dreams of the baker, the butler, and ultimately Pharaoh.

–   *He solved a problem and was promoted* - Pharaoh had a dream that no one could interpret. The butler and chief baker remembered Joseph and told Pharaoh about him. Joseph interpreted the dream and advised Pharaoh as to how to approach the upcoming famine and Pharaoh responded. The famine came as Joseph interpreted and ultimately, Pharaoh promoted Joseph to be second in command over all of Egypt. Because of the famine, his family came to him seeking to purchase food. His family didn't recognize him as they made obeisance to him. Little did they know, as they approached him and bowed before him, Joseph's dream was coming to pass (See chapters 39-45). He was blessed! Why was he blessed? Because: 1. The Lord was with him and 2. Everything Joseph did and touched, God made it prosper. Regardless to those major setbacks, God still wasn't finished with him. His life wasn't over, his assignment was not aborted. Everything that took place in Joseph's life led to the ultimate promotion.

Throughout Joseph's experiences, he stayed mindful of what God showed him in the dream. He didn't understand why he experienced those situations but regardless to what happened to him, he never let go of the dream. Some of you reading this right now, may have had a dream given to you by God and situations arose over the years to try to discourage you from continuing on the path laid out for you. You may have been passed over for a number of promotions; I did; but I'm here to tell you that as long as you stay mindful of the ultimate reason you're still doing that job – to glorify God – the reward **will** come. And you can take that to the bank!

All Joseph knew was that he dreamed a dream; he didn't know how his dream was going to come into fruition; he just believed and continued to put his hands to work on whatever he was given to do. Throughout all of his experiences from childhood to adulthood, his perspective and willingness to endure helped him to see his destiny fulfilled. Sure, being chased by a woman, lied on, and then thrown in jail all took him outside of his comfort zone – the challenges we've faced on our jobs as we tried to serve the Lord have taken us outside of our comfort zones – but when you make the decision to serve the Lord and please Him, it's never easy or simple. You don't just walk a straight path. On the contrary, there are curves, hills, ditches, pot holes, some dead ends, and speed bumps, along your path to pleasing God. It's never a boring trip to say the least. The only thing you have to do is decide you're not going to quit no matter what comes your way. You have to decide that you're going to serve the Lord until your assignment's been completed!

Colossians 3 says that if you're serious about this life (style); if you're serious about being led by the Holy Spirit, pursue those things (that pertain to life and godliness). Don't accept the status quo or business as usual. Those things aren't acceptable to God. It's a higher way of living and working and that will bring God glory. That's what Joseph did.

CHAPTER 6

Bearing One Another's Burdens (and so fulfill the law of Christ)

When the Holy Spirit gave me the title of this chapter, I thought I had an idea of what he wanted to convey but it has taken on a different perspective.

I realize that every manager, boss, or executive may not be a Christian or as spiritually mature and this chapter is for those assistants who work with them. I'm sure there have been challenges and opportunities that presented themselves as you, the spirit-led assistant tried to be obedient to the Holy Spirit and still make your boss look good. I'm sure there were days where you thought that you couldn't take any more of the foolishness, abuse, politics, etc. but for some reason, you couldn't leave and weren't too sure why. The Holy Spirit compelled you to stay because of the bigger picture; because there was something He wanted to do, somebody He wanted to reach, and the only way He could that have access, was through you. Your demeanor, conversations, and work performance all became instrumental in God working strategically in that organization, department, and office.

You may be working for a boss right now and it is clearly evident that you are more qualified than he is. I understand the frustrations you have experienced. I understand the questions you've asked. I understand the problems all of this has created; I've worked in similar situations myself. Romans 15:1-6 Amplified gives us the response to this:

"We who are strong [in our convictions and of robust faith] ought to bear with the failings and the frailties and the tender scruples of the weak; [we ought to help carry the doubts and qualms of others] and not to please ourselves. Let each one of us make it a practice to please (make happy) his neighbor for his good *and* for his true welfare, to edify him [to strengthen him and build him up spiritually]. For Christ did not please Himself [gave no thought to His own interests] but, as it is written, 'The reproaches *and* abuses of those who reproached *and* abused you fell on Me. For whatever was **thus written in former days was written for our instruction, that by [our steadfast and patient] endurance and the encouragement [drawn] from the Scriptures we might hold fast to *and* cherish hope.** Now may the God Who gives power of patient endurance (steadfastness) and Who supplies encouragement, grant you to live in such mutual harmony *and* such full sympathy with one another, in accord with Christ Jesus. That together you may [unanimously] with united hearts *and* one voice, praise and glorify the God and Father of our Lord Jesus Christ (the Messiah)."

The Message says it like this:

"Those of us who are strong and able in the faith need to step in and lend a hand to those who falter, and not just do what is most convenient for us. *Strength is for service, not status*. Each one of us needs to look after the good of the people around us, asking ourselves, 'How can I help?' That's exactly what Jesus did. He didn't make it easy for himself by avoiding people's troubles, but waded right in and helped out. 'I took on the troubles of the troubled,' is the way Scripture puts it. Even if it was written in Scripture long ago, you can be sure it's written for *us*. God wants the combination of his steady, constant calling and warm, personal counsel in Scripture to come to characterize *us*, keeping us alert for whatever he will do next. May our dependably steady and warmly personal God develop maturity in you so that you get along with each other as well as Jesus gets along with us all."

As assistants, we all bring a wealth of information, skills, and knowledge to our positions. Some of us may have specific certifications, degrees, in addition to experience and all that together can intimidate our boss if we don't put it all into its proper perspective. As I shared in an earlier chapter and The Message version of Romans 15 confirmed it for me, **Strength is for service, not status.** I remember an interview I had with a potential employer and I shared with that I've always approached my job with the objective of adding my strength to my boss and/or department. I made a decision a long time ago that whatever he was confronted with, so was I and together, we were going to work through the assignment, task, problem, whatever it was, I had by boss' back and they knew it.

By adding your strength – your skills, abilities, education and most importantly, your attitude and willingness – you will be able to work with a boss who may not be qualified for the position he's in...and you both know it. Continue to respect the position the person holds and communicate with him from that aspect. No matter how challenging that boss is or becomes, allow the Holy Spirit to give you wisdom and discernment in working with him. By doing this, you will learn to "cover" your boss' weakness. You will be amazed at how things turn out. Not being moved by your boss' shortcomings, you present an opportunity for God to come on the scene and be glorified – your boss perceives you differently and trust unfolds at another level. Confidence builds – in you and your boss – and the atmosphere in the office is changed for the better because everyone feels good; no one is embarrassed by having their shortcoming exposed for others to see. Am I looking at this scenario through rose colored glasses? No, even in those instances when there's no outward acknowledgement of your efforts to be a blessing to your boss, he knows what you did.

Bearing one another's burdens simply means that we are to cover one another. We are to help, assist, and aid another during their time of vulnerability. We do so because we are keeping the overall objective in mind of what we are trying to accomplish. We are focused on the outcome that we come alongside to assist and add our strength to whatever area has been identified as having a weakness. I still hear about how my current boss wouldn't answer emails. Communicating with him by email meant that your email was going into the "email abyss." The funny thing about it is that I had no idea that people had challenges getting email responses from him before I came. When I came into the position, I knew he needed to be aware of EVERYTHING PERTINENT. I created a folder of those emails he needed to be cognizant of and had hard copies in that folder. Once he saw them, he could respond appropriately and follow up with people as he needed. How did I know he had a weakness? In that aspect I didn't know because I was already adding my strength by keeping him informed. When did I know it was a weakness? When people came to me and thanked me for being his assistant and shared that story with me.

Creating a folder for emails and other correspondence was a strategy from the Holy Ghost. I didn't know he wasn't always prompt in responding or communicating to others via email, but God did. As I position myself to do this job as unto the Lord, I also position myself to hear from the Holy Spirit and He gives me ideas, strategies, and instructions that will lighten the burden my boss has. He'll do the same for you.

As spirit-let assistants, it pleases God when we step in and take up any slack our boss has. He's pleased even more when we do it willingly. I make this statement because I know firsthand about working with and for a difficult boss. I'm sure you can think of one...or two that you've worked for as well. As you began and continued to work alongside your boss, you learned that you both had a different approach, a different perspective in how you were to perform your job. Where you are looking at ways to make it seamless not only for yourself but you're your boss as well. Instead of welcoming your efforts, it seems that any response from the boss is to thwart and seemingly sabotage your work. It doesn't matter that you're both on the same team – at least you thought you were. No matter how much you pray and get direction and follow those instructions, something else comes along and frustrates you more and more.

If you're like me, you work ethic defines you and a part of that definition is your professionalism and respect towards your superiors....and do your job well. You continue in that mindset, no matter how much grief and frustration your boss creates for you. A spirit-led assistant is always following the Holy Spirit and He reveals the next step, the next place for you a little at a time. Because we are always focused on doing our jobs well, we may not realize that we may have gotten comfortable or become complacent (to a degree) in that position and that particular boss may be in our lives to provoke us to begin seeking God for the next phase in our lives. The bible states that we should go from glory to glory; we should never become stagnant. Our lives should be an active display of God-likeness through our behavior, attitude, and actions. This means that there should be physical evidence that we are Christians.

As we follow the Holy Spirit's direction, the situation may eventually reveal itself in a physical change – one where you're moving onto another position, your boss moving on, or both of you moving on. I've come to learn that whenever I have been frustrated in a position and it's lasted over a period of time, it takes me deeper into prayer and study of the scriptures. While doing this, I keep my inner ear open to hear the voice of the Lord and get instructions that move me further on the path God has set me on.

As I'm seeking Him, I'm still working and performing my job as unto the Lord; I still want Him to be glorified in this difficult situation. In spite of all of the opposition, I'm still looking to God and praying for ways to please Him so that I could "complete" that job. While following the path, an unexpected twist comes and brings promotion. It's then you realize how God was orchestrating behind the scenes all along....

As you remain open and teachable, and still performing your job unto the Lord; and as you cover your boss' weakness, the Holy Spirit will set you up for promotion. Just for clarity, I'm not saying that promotion comes because of his weakness. On the contrary, promotion comes as a result of your decision to honor and respect your boss by covering those weaknesses. Another thing I want to interject here is that promotion comes from the Lord, not man. The Lord establishes who He wants to put in place. He sets people up and He pulls down those who will not listen to Him. You may not completely agree with my statements but once you realize (that what I have been saying in this book) that as children of God, we operate, function, and live in a totally different system than those who don't know the Lord. We work among men but our issues are never with them. Our issues are spiritual in nature and show up in our physical (senses) realm. "For we wrestle not against flesh and blood but against principalities, against powers, against rulers of the darkness..." (Ephesians 6:12). Our fight, challenge, opposition, isn't always a person, but usually a spirit influencing the person, as a response to you. We are not of this world, this physical realm, but we are of the Kingdom of God. Where is this kingdom, you ask? Jesus said the kingdom is in us. It's in us because we are spirit beings, first and foremost. The world is intrigued by the occult and supernatural phenomena, and as children of God, we need to be intrigued by the Kingdom of God! The Kingdom of God is a lifestyle, an attitude, a way of living that is contrary to what is popular, convenient, or acceptable to the world or today's society. Example of a kingdom 'concept': when you are mistreated by someone, your "natural" response is to get back at them, to retaliate. Jesus said in Matthew 5:44, "Love your enemies, bless them that curse you, do good to them that hate you, and pray for them which despitefully use you, and persecute you...." This goes totally against present-day societal norms!

We've had bosses (and co-workers) who mistreated us, tried to take advantage of us. They've talked about us, lied on us, tried to do whatever they could to make our lives difficult and they seemed to get pleasure out of trying to make our lives miserable! Your response to their actions was informing your boss of the incident(s), conflict mediation, confronting them, all the way to reporting to Human Resources; following all of the proper channels and creating the paper trails and none of it brought about an acceptable resolution. You may have gotten demoted, transferred, or outright terminated as a result. As a child of God, He wants us to trust Him for those who mistreat you. An Old Testament term for God as our avenger is "Jehovah-G'molah. He will avenge us of those who mistreat us. In the meantime, we are to do two things and that is continue to love them and pray for them. You are probably ready to close this book and disregard everything I've said up to this point. You're probably thinking, "this girl has lost her mind! Where DID she come from??? I've never heard anything like this before!" You may be using a few "choice" words right now and believe me, I understand completely! I responded the same way when Holy Spirit instructed me to do the same thing I'm sharing with you! I am not saying anything to you that I haven't had to do myself!

The bottom line is this: In allowing the Holy Spirit to have permission to change how I conducted myself on my job, I had to learn to take the high road; I had to be the mature one. It forced me to grow up and show others there was another way, a better way to conduct ourselves in a professional setting. The Message version of Matthew 23:11 explains it best:

"If someone takes unfair advantage of you, use the occasion to practice the servant life. No more tit-for-tat stuff. Live generously." Jesus goes on further to say that He's challenging our former ways of thinking, "I'm telling you to love your enemies. Let them bring out the best in you, not the worst. When someone gives you a hard time, respond with the energies of prayer, for then you are working out of your **true** selves, your God-created selves. This is what God does – He gives His best – the sun to warm and rain to nourish – to everyone, regardless: the good and bad, the nice and nasty. If all you do is love the lovable, do you expect a bonus? Anybody can do that. If you simply say hello to those who greet you, do you expect a medal? Any run-of-the-mill sinner can do that. In a word, what I'm saying is, **_Grow up. You're Kingdom subjects. Now live like it. Live out of your God-created identity._** Live generously and graciously toward others, the way God lives towards you." WOW!!! (emphasis mine)

Jesus knew we'd experience incompetent bosses and coworkers. He came to bring healing and wholeness back into our lives and to do that, He had to establish a completely different system than what people have been accustomed to. He knew people would be functioning out of a place of brokenness. Something's broken in their lives and they communicate from that broken place. Our response to them is to love and pray for them and God will help us do that. As we do this, our work performance goes to another level. We may offer to take on additional responsibilities, offer to train the person, or give suggestions to make their job easier. In other words, we lend a hand willingly because we do it out of service to our Lord. Praise God!

Still not convinced? Romans 12:2 in the Message puts it this way, "....take your everyday, ordinary life – your sleeping, eating, going-to-work, and walking-around life – and place it before God as an offering. Embracing what God does for you is the best thing you can do for him. Don't become so well-adjusted to your culture that you fit into it without even thinking. Instead, fix your attention on God. <u>You'll be changed from the inside out</u>. ***Readily recognize what he wants from you, and quickly respond to it.*** Unlike the culture around you, always dragging you down to its level of immaturity, ***God brings the best out of you, develops well-formed maturity in you."*** Enough said.

CHAPTER 7

Your Assignment
(Called, chosen, equipped)

I have been honored that every promotion I've been blessed with, each position was CREATED. Outside of the position I worked in at the bank, each position was created and I never saw it coming. When I interviewed for a couple of Executive Assistant positions in the past, although I met the job qualifications, I didn't get the job due to seniority or politics. At one point, I stopped applying for positions unless the Holy Spirit said to apply. In another instance He told me to apply for a position and after I got that job, I was automatically promoted to another position a few months later.

I have been fortunate to work for bosses who allowed me to develop and flourish in my position. Whether it was through their encouragement (or lack thereof), I always sought the Holy Spirit in performing my jobs. As I look back over each chapter, I realize that the examples given have taken place in my life to some degree and all of it collectively, prepared me for writing this book. Because I made the conscious decision to perform all of my jobs "heartily" as unto the Lord, I positioned myself to be receptive to His leading and direction. I realized that He CALLED me to be a support, a help to each administrator, manager, executive I've worked with and He has EQUIPPED me through a number of ways. Whether it was by attending classes, workshops, seminars, on-the-job training, it was all done as HE directed me. I didn't take classes unless I believed He led me to go to school. Even when obstacles came to try to block me and any future progress to be made, the Holy Spirit used those situations to teach me. I've worked with bad managers before and His primary instruction was to keep working, keep doing my job unto Him. Every job was performed to please God and give Him the glory. I didn't want any recognition and when it did come, it was in the form of a promotion.

Because I chose to glorify God, He CHOSE me to ultimately serve in the capacity I'm in presently. At the time of writing this book, I received a promotion that again, I didn't see coming. Because of my desire to be a bigger, better blessing to my boss, the ministry, my Pastors, and the Kingdom of God; I'd pray consistently for ways to be a blessing and the bible states that as I delight myself in The Lord, He will give me the desires of my heart. This means that as I delight myself; make myself happy, He would grant the secret petitions of my heart. It also means that He would exchange my desires for His desires. In other words, God's desires became my desires. In this instance, the desire to be a bigger impact towards helping to achieve my boss' objectives, was a desire that came from God because it was going to help fulfill the vision of our CEO and the organization.

Since I began writing this book, God blessed me with another promotion. It was another created position: Senior Executive Assistant. In this position, I've been given authority to respond on behalf of my director when he is out of the office. This means that he has entrusted to me a certain level of authority on different matters and respond as he would respond. When I think about it, the only other person who has another assistant like me, IS THE CEO! I am honored and humbled because I know that all the work I've put forth over the years has resulted in this promotion. I serve the living God and my focus is always to please Him. I know that I please God by pleasing my boss.

What is a Spirit-led Assistant? (S)He is one who is a part of the Ministry of Helps and operates primarily with the gift of administration. 1 Corinthians 12:4-11 talks about the diversities, administrations, and operations of the Holy Spirit. I like how the Message translation spells it out: "God's various gifts are handed out everywhere, but they all originate in God's Spirit. God's various ministries are carried out everywhere; but they all originate in God's Spirit. God's various expressions of power are in action everywhere; but God Himself is behind it all. ***Each person is given something to do that shows who God is***: Everyone gets in on it, everyone benefits." We have the opportunity and honor to show who God is as spirit-led assistants! Hallelujah!

In other words, it is God who works in and through us. He is the Author and Finisher of our faith; He is the beginning and the end. When we decide to become a Spirit-led Assistant, it all starts and ends with God. The good thing about being a Spirit-led Assistant? Because we trust Him, looking to Him to give us the answers, the pressure is on Him to perform and not on us. It is not by my efforts, my ideas, my skills that I depend on alone to work my job. I don't rely on any of those things. Sometimes I have mental blocks and get frustrated trying to figure things out by myself. I have to lean on God's infinite wisdom and trust Him to work through me. There have been a number of times I've said, "Lord, this is a job for You. If You don't do it, it won't get done". And you know what? He always responds! How, you ask? In the quality of work that's completed. By how a situation was resolved. The way a complaint has been handled and the guest's needs were met above and beyond their expectations. By meeting a deadline way ahead of schedule.

As you begin to reevaluate your performance, my prayer is that you decide to become a Spirit-led Assistant. The journey is exciting; there's never a dull moment when following the leading of the Holy Spirit. Your job becomes more exciting because you're now taken outside your comfort zone. He will challenge you, teach you, encourage you, and correct you, to ultimately promote you.

Colossians 3:23,24 Amplified version, sums it up this way: "Whatever may be your task, work at it heartily (from the soul), as something done for The Lord and not for men, Knowing [with **ALL** certainty] that it is from The Lord [and not from men] that you will receive the inheritance which is your [real] reward. [The One Whom] you are actually serving [is] The Lord Christ (the Messiah)." (Capitalization mine). As you fulfill your assignment heartily, to completion, your reward is ultimately coming from above. As you remain humble, by staying receptive to the Holy Spirit's leading, you eventually get exalted by God Himself. Your gift will make room for you and will always manifest in promotion. I am a living witness and it's only by His grace and mercy that I write these words to you, the reader.

If you've ever questioned your legitimacy in the position you are currently occupying, please know that you have been Called to serve and support, you have been Chosen by God Himself to walk alongside your boss, and you have been Equipped by the Holy Ghost to complete the assignment given to you. God wants to use you because He's placed gifts, talents, skills, and abilities inside of you in order to get the job done right where you are! The classes you've taken, the degree you may have, all have been accomplished in order to fulfill the will of God in this season of your life. You may be one of those persons who obtained a degree and not using it at all but God allowed you to achieve that milestone to bring about a level of discipline that you're now using in your current position. Nothing is wasted, everything you have experienced and accomplished in your work life has all brought you to this place at this time and season. Nothing is too hard, nothing is impossible; you CAN do ALL things through Jesus Christ who gives you the strength. His power, his ability is inside you and because it is, there is no way you can fail! Praise God!

You are a prime example of the grace of God manifesting in your life because it shows up through relationship. Your focus is not on pleasing man but pleasing God. You please God by pleasing your boss.

Lastly, I've given you spiritual insights but I also showed where I did some "natural" things that I did physically that helped me become a spirit-led assistant. I love learning and have become somewhat of a professional student. I have always taken a class, attended a workshop or seminar that has helped improve my skills. At work, there were times I offered to take on projects as a way to bring to the surface any "hidden" skills. In these times, I would be impressed as I saw the results of the Holy Spirit's leading. (Yes, I said 'impressed'. Sometimes I impress myself because I didn't know a particular talent was in me until Holy Spirit brought it to the surface.) As I stated in the introduction, I was seeking ways to improve, develop and grow, when I was introduced to the term, "Managing Up."

CHAPTER 8

Final Words

Everything that has been written is not possible without an on-going relationship with Christ. If we pay attention to how Jesus operated, we come to see that everything He did was motivated by LOVE.... His love for the people; wanting them to do and have much better than their current state.

The bible states in Matthew 4:23 that while Jesus was in a certain location, he healed every disease, sickness, and infirmity among the people. He also shared the good news of the Gospel. My point is that He set Himself, He actively engaged every part of His being to improve the quality of life of the people He came in contact with. As assistants, we should always position ourselves to improve our work environment – by the conversations we have with our bosses and team members, as well in the quality of work we put forth on a daily basis. Jesus was compelled to do good, let that same motivation be found in us. Let us be that team player as well. (Hebrews 10:24).

Some of you may be wondering why I decided to write this book. Truthfully, I had no idea I would be writing this book, but God did. This book was written (and future ones) because there is a way God wants to affect and influence the work place that is totally different than what we are accustomed to. We can attend school and get all sorts of college degrees and certifications, attend all sorts of seminars, and all of that is great. I've done the same thing over the course of my adult life. The principles and lessons taught are good and they work but I've learned that until our minds have been changed or renewed, those same principles and lessons won't work effectively. The beginning of the book began with Colossians 3:24-27 with particular emphasis on verse 23: "And whatsoever you do, do it heartily, as unto the Lord, and not unto man..." The word "heartily" as stated before means "spirit, breath" in Greek. I literally depend on God speaking to me as to how to do my job. I depend on His directions, wisdom, ideas to help me do my job. I want to look at the word "reward" from this same passage. It literally means "inheritance" in the Greek translation. I've been speaking of reward in the form of promotion and "inheritance" is an expansion of promotion. I don't want to get into a lot of detail as I want to expand on this in the next book but I do want the reader to understand that there is an inheritance we have because of our relationship with Jesus Christ. The bible states that we are heirs of God and joint-heirs with Jesus. This means that because we are associated with Him out of relationship, we are entitled to receive something substantial at the appointed time. In the world's system, this inheritance usually comes at the death of a loved one and is spelled out in a will and testament. Because Jesus died in order to reconcile man back to God, we inherit eternal life when we accept and receive Jesus as our Savior. What a lot of people do not realize is that although we receive eternal life, we also receive some "perks", "benefits" while we are still living this life. Making the decision to obey this scripture took me to another level in my work performance. I began to realize gifts and talents that have been resident inside me were always there; I just didn't know that they existed. It also revealed a level of creativity, a level of "heart" that I didn't know I had. I'm sure you have heard the phrase: "He has a lot of heart." There is a passion, determination, perseverance that I didn't know I had. I am always looking for ways to expand myself in order to be a bigger help to my boss. It has ultimately taken me to a place called Grace – a place of blessing – God's enabling power to succeed and prosper. It took me to a place of functioning at a level I didn't really know existed: to a level inside the Kingdom of God because I was working and doing tasks as I was led, instructed, and directed by the Holy Spirit. God wants all of us to operate at this level. It goes totally against the way business and corporate America operate business but in doing so, it releases a level of prosperity and blessing that comes from God. Your reward or inheritance goes way beyond the pay check.

The blessing of becoming a Spirit-Led Assistant? Let's look at my highlights from earlier and compare:

Managing Up	Spirit-Led Assistant
1. Pay attention to your boss' needs	Develop the attitude of a servant
2. It's proactive and will seek out ways to improve processes and the workplace	Seek to please God. Motivation is pleasing God.
3. Become a team player-doing whatever it takes to get the job done	Allow Holy Spirit to take you outside of your comfort zone by blessing those who are less than capable of performing their assigned tasks
4. Your needs are met when your boss' needs are met	You're more concerned about the will of God. His desires become your desires.
5. It's a way to make you stand out in the workplace.	Because your attitude and disposition is pleasing God first, His response to you is always promotion.

The outcomes are very similar and I'm not out to discount or minimize the concept of Managing Up. What I am trying to convey and I hope as the reader, you were able to grasp, is that as a spirit-led assistant, your entire life should be one that's spirit-led and spirit-driven. Everything about you should show that your lifestyle has its influences that are God-breathed. Your life should always be fresh, alive, and attractive to others. Your job is just one component of who you are as a whole; it should be evident that you have a relationship with Jesus Christ in everything you do.

Managing Up: Doing It God's Way takes you beyond the status quo. It expands your capacity from the inside out. As you become sensitive to the leading of the Holy Spirit, your capacity to receive from Him is expanded. This has become my prayer recently. The instructions, wisdom, the answers I get from Him has literally left me dumbfounded at times. They have been things that I could not have come up with even if I spent countless hours trying to. The responses have been simple, easy, and left me feeling a sense of satisfaction after completing the assignment. There has been an ease in performing most assignments and tasks.

God wants to challenge you in becoming an assistant who's led by Him. It really is not difficult, it's just a matter of settling yourself inwardly so that you can hear Him with your inner ear. It's taking the time to do so. It's breaking away from the current way of doing things and let Him organize and possibly prioritize our work loads. As assistants, we look for immediate results, actively search for solutions. We are solutions-oriented or problem solvers. I thank God that by learning to wait and listen to him, I get the best solutions and He gets the glory. He wants to be glorified in your work performance. Give Him that opportunity and I promise you, you won't be disappointed.

Questions to Ask to Help You Understand
Managing Up – God's Way

1. When you hear the term, "servant", what do you think about?
2. Define "submission." How does your definition of submission fit the book's definition?
3. Do you have a personal relationship with God? Define your relationship.
4. Do you know the vision/mission of your organization? Can you write/repeat it?
5. How well do you know your boss? Can you define his/her personality?
6. Define your personality. Compare and contrast your personality with that of your boss. Do you clash or gel with your boss?
7. What are your goals? Short and long-term?
8. Does your company promote personal growth and development? Does your boss encourage growth and development for your job?
9. Do you seek out opportunities for further growth and development? What have been those opportunities?
10. What is it that you really want? What drives you? What motivates you?

These questions are a barometer of where you are in the process of Managing Up God's Way. They will help give you an idea of areas you may need to make any adjustments in order to become a spirit-led assistant.

Bibliography (Resources)

Online:

Dictionary.com

Blog.penelopetrunk.com. "7 Ways to Manage Up". November 3, 2006.

Www.govloop.com. "Managing Up - What Does It Mean and Why Is Everyone Talking About It?" October 26, 2012.

Www.tlnt.com. "Managing Up: What the Heck Is It and Why Should You Care?" August 6, 2013.

Online.wsj.com. "What It Means to Manage Up". October 30, 2008.

Www.biblegateway.com/resources/Matthew-henry/ Col.3.18-Col.3:25

Books:

Badowski, Rosanne. Managing Up. Currency Books, a division of Random House, New York, New York. 2003.

Strong, James, S.T.D., L.L.D. Strong's Exhaustive Concordance Compact Edition. Baker Book House, Grand Rapids Michigan, 1992.

Notes

Venita L. Blakely

Biography

As a 2010 recipient of *Strathmore's Who's Who in Executive Leadership* in addition to receiving an award for *Executive Professionals*, Venita has distinguished herself as the "go-to" person when it comes to demonstrating what a quality Executive Assistant is all about.

No matter what industry she finds herself in, Venita has always exhibited the traits and attributes that set her apart from her colleagues. Her attitude has always been to go into the workplace with the intent of improving and/or streamlining existing processes with the ultimate purpose of adding her strength to whomever she is working with. Venita approaches each position she has ever worked in as an assignment and the outcome shows just that. Her demeanor is consistent in that she conveys a warmth, an authenticity and still remain professional which makes it a pleasure to work with. Because she enjoys what she does, Venita is always exploring new ways to enhance her skills.

As a "Baby Boomer", it has been stated that before this generation finally retires, its members will work in 3 – 5 careers. Venita is currently in her 4th career, previously working in banking, manufacturing, education, and now full-time ministry. She is the proud mother of 2 adult children and 2 granddaughters, Eden and Mercy. She resides in the metro Atlanta Georgia area.

Printed in the United States
By Bookmasters